# UNDERSTANDING
# COMPUTER SAFETY

Paul Mason

raintree

a Capstone company — publishers for children

Raintree is an imprint of Capstone Global Library Limited, a company incorporated in England and Wales having its registered office at 7 Pilgrim Street, London, EC4V 6LB – Registered company number: 6695582

www.raintreepublishers.co.uk
myorders@raintreepublishers.co.uk

Edited by Linda Staniford and Chris Harbo
Designed by Richard Parker and Tim Bond
Original illustrations © Capstone Global Library 2015
Illustrated by Nigel Dobbyn (Beehive Illustration)
Picture research by Jo Miller
Production by Victoria Fitzgerald
Originated by Capstone Global Library Ltd
Printed and bound in China by CTPS

ISBN 978 1 406 28977 0
18 17 16 15 14
10 9 8 7 6 5 4 3 2 1

British Library Cataloguing in Publication Data
A full catalogue record for this book is available from the British Library.

Acknowledgements
We would like to thank the following for permission to reproduce photographs:

Alamy: ©imageBROKER, 16, ©Isabelle Plasschaert, 39, ©Marmaduke St. John, 40, ©maximimages.com, 17 left and right, ©NUAGE, 31, ©Oote Boe Photography, 20; Corbis: ©Ann Summa, 4, Blend Images/©Kevin Dodge, 18, ©Stefanie Grewel, 42; Dreamstime©Dragonimages, 15; Getty Images: Altrendo/altrendo images, 5, flickr Editorial/Moment Mobile /Hattanas Kumcha, 24; iStockphoto: ©daizuoxin, 14, ©PacoRomero, 7, © Vesnaandjic, 6, ©Yuri_Arcurs, 8; Shutterstock:areeya_ann, 37, Alexey Boldin, 13, Blend Images, 26, Goodluz, 36, Martin Novak, 22, Monkey Business Images, 43, racorn, 25, tab62, 30, T.W. van Urk, 10, Viktoria Kazakova, cover; SuperStock: agefotostock, 38. Design Elements: Shutterstock: HunThomas, vectorlib.com (throughout)

We would like to thank Andrew Connell for his invaluable help in the preparation of this book.

Every effort has been made to contact copyright holders of material reproduced in this book. Any omissions will be rectified in subsequent printings if notice is given to the publisher.

All the internet addresses (URLs) given in this book were valid at the time of going to press. However, due to the dynamic nature of the internet, some addresses may have changed, or sites may have changed or ceased to exist since publication. While the author and publisher regret any inconvenience this may cause readers, no responsibility for any such changes can be accepted by either the author or the publisher.

# CONTENTS

Some words are shown in bold, **like this.** You can find out what they mean by looking in the glossary.

# INTRODUCTION: WHAT IS COMPUTER SAFETY?

▲Computers are great fun - but they can also lead you into danger.
This book will help you learn how to use computers safely.

Computer safety means keeping yourself safe from the dangerous people and risky situations that are part of the world of computers. It does NOT mean being careful to avoid dropping a heavy computer on your foot – though you should do that too!

## The digital world

The world of computers is often called the **digital** world. People sometimes think the digital world and the real world are separate. But the digital world and real life are connected. The dangers of the digital world can be just as real as those you meet in real life.

# COMPUTER FUTURE

Computers have already led to changes that people would not have believed possible 20 years ago. Back then, there were no smartphones or tablets. Even the first iPod only appeared in 2001!

## Danger in the digital world

Just like in real life (which computer users sometimes call **IRL**), the main danger in the digital world comes from people who are dishonest. They might be lying to steal money, or because they want to do harm in some other way. It is these people that computer users have to keep themselves safe from.

▲Would you talk to a stranger in real life? A good first safety rule for computer users is not to do anything in the virtual world they would not do in the real world.

## DO'S AND DON'TS

DO: Make sure you understand how computers and the internet work together

DON'T: Just assume that everything to do with the internet is safe and alright

# COMPUTER FUTURE

Some futurists think that one day soon, a lot of the information on the internet will come from non-human sources. This is known as the Internet of Things. One example would be a basketball containing a computer chip, which sends a signal to the TV every time it is bounced. The chip would warn the TV that there is a basketball player nearby. The TV would then record any basketball games that are being shown.

▲Imagine if your fridge could order more milk when you ran low. The Internet of Things will make this a reality.

## Computers and the internet

Almost all computers use the internet. The internet is a network of computers that covers almost the whole world. It allows computers to communicate with each other.

One way to imagine the internet is as a kind of computer-based postal service. People send little packets of information using the internet, a bit like sending little packets containing letters in the post. The internet is much faster than the post, though. Letters take days to arrive, but the internet takes fractions of a second to deliver information.

## False information

Almost anyone who has a computer can connect to the internet and **download** information. They can also **upload** information. Often, no one checks if what has been uploaded is true. False information can stay on a **website** for years without being corrected. Sometimes people even copy it and spread it to other websites.

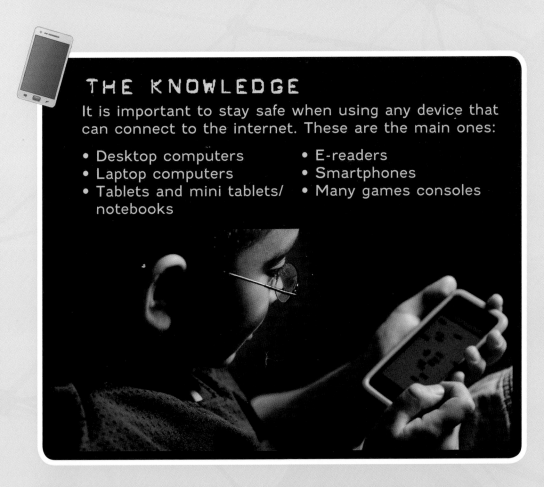

### THE KNOWLEDGE

It is important to stay safe when using any device that can connect to the internet. These are the main ones:

- Desktop computers
- Laptop computers
- Tablets and mini tablets/ notebooks
- E-readers
- Smartphones
- Many games consoles

# The internet vs the World Wide Web

The internet is different from the World Wide Web (though people often think they are the same thing). The internet is a global network of computers. Together, the websites on this network that store information are called the World Wide Web.

# CHAPTER 1: WHAT IS THE DIFFERENCE BETWEEN ONLINE AND OFFLINE?

When a computer is not connected to the internet it is **offline**. When it is connected, it is **online**. Computer safety is especially important when a computer is online, or could later go online. So, knowing whether your computer is online or offline is important.

▲Smartphones can do all kinds of jobs – including sending photos to the internet.

### THE KNOWLEDGE

Computers store information in two main places. They store some information inside the computer, where it is always available. But they also use the internet to store information on other computers. This second kind of storage is often called **cloud storage**.

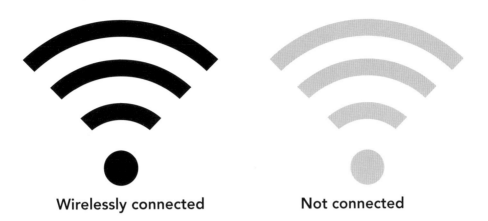

**Wirelessly connected**          **Not connected**

It is easy to tell if a computer is wirelessly connected to the internet: somewhere on the screen, this symbol will be black. If the symbol is grey, the computer is not connected.

# How computers connect to the internet

Most computers connect to the internet using two devices: a **modem** and a **router**. Sometimes, both are contained in one case and they look like a single device.

There are two main ways for the computer to get information from the modem/router:

1. In a hard-wired connection, a cable connects the computer to the modem/router.

2. In a **wireless** connection, the computer connects to a wireless router without the need for cables.

Smartphones and some tablets can also connect to the internet wirelessly using the mobile-phone network, instead of a wireless router. It is possible to stop this happening by turning off "cellular data" or "mobile data" in the phone's **settings**.

# Offline computing

Almost all computers will work when they are offline. Lots of **software** programmes are stored in a computer's memory, and do not need an internet connection to work. For example, writing reports, playing some games, looking at photos, making a cartoon with your friends, and creating music playlists can all be done offline.

An offline computer is like a person sitting in a room on his or her own. In theory disaster *could* strike: there could be an earthquake, hurricane, or gas explosion, for example. In general, though, someone sitting alone in a room is unlikely to come to much harm. In the same way, an offline computer is on its own, and safe from people using other computers to attack it.

## DO'S AND DON'TS

DO: Remember that even if you are offline, your work might later be shared online

DON'T: Share things that might offend someone or get you into trouble

▲Careful! Would you really want this image to fall into the wrong hands?

# COMPUTER FUTURE

Some futurists think that one day soon, people's homes and other possessions will be constantly feeding information to the Internet of Things (see panel on page 6). These devices will NEVER be offline.

## Permanently offline vs offline for now

Some computer programmes allow you to work offline, then send information to the internet once the computer is online again. Email works like this. You can write an email offline, but if you click "send" while the computer is offline, the email is stored in the outbox. As soon as the computer is online, it sends out your mail without even being asked. Computers send and receive information in this way, all the time, without being asked.

**Offline permanently**          **Offline temporarily**          **Online**

# Online computing

Lots of the things that make computers useful rely on being online. Sending and receiving mails, researching the exact date of your favourite band's first number-one hit, some games, and **chat rooms**, for example, all need an internet connection.

A computer that goes online is like a person who's been in their room alone and then decides to go to the park. There's a lot more to do in the park, but there are also more things that could go wrong. You could fall off the swings, crash your bike, meet someone unpleasant, or get in an argument with your friend. In the same way, an online computer offers the chance of lots of different activities, but also added dangers.

## THE KNOWLEDGE

Internet filters are a way of stopping **illegal**, upsetting or **inappropriate** information being downloaded from the internet. They are used by all kinds of people, ranging from governments to parents. It is almost impossible to make a completely reliable filter, because if the controls are too tight, harmless information will also be blocked. So even on a computer with filters, it is still important to follow the rules of computer safety.

# COMPUTER FUTURE

Wearables are small computer devices that are worn under, in or attached to clothing. One example is wristwatch-like devices like the one shown here, which constantly feed information to and from the internet. Another is running shoes that download training times and other information.

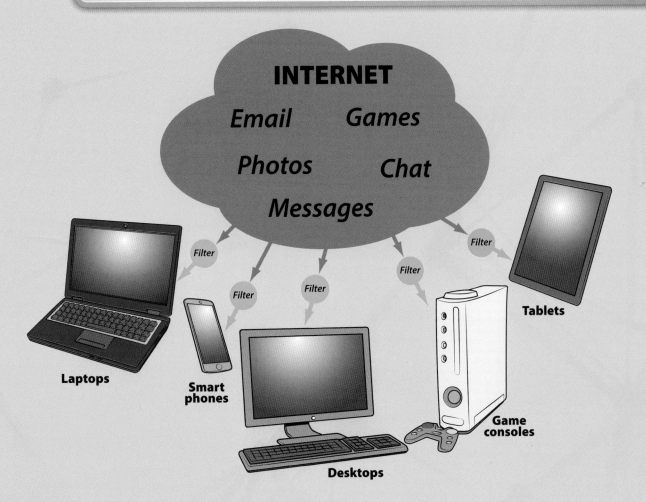

**INTERNET**

*Email*      *Games*

*Photos*      *Chat*

*Messages*

Filter    Filter    Filter    Filter    Filter

**Laptops**

**Smart phones**

**Desktops**

**Game consoles**

**Tablets**

▲Being online gives access to the internet, and connects you to other computer users. Filters can stop some unwanted information from getting through.

13

# CHAPTER 2: WHAT ARE DIGITAL FOOTPRINTS?

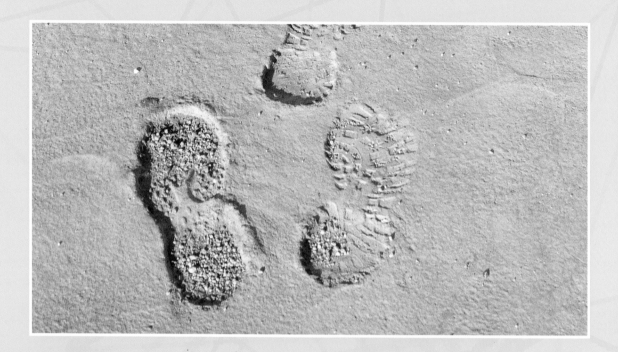

A digital footprint is the evidence someone leaves behind as they pass through the digital world. Digital footprints are like footprints left in concrete: once they are there, they are very difficult to rub out completely!

## THE KNOWLEDGE

IP stands for "Internet Protocol". All computers that use the internet have an IP address. It works a bit like a postal address, telling other computers on the internet where information should be delivered and where it has come from. IP addresses are like fingerprints: no two are the same.

▲Almost everything you do on a computer adds to your digital footprint.

## What makes up a digital footprint?

A digital footprint is made up of information about how someone behaves online. It might include what they have searched for on the internet, pages they have visited, items they have bought, things they have "liked", their location and the kinds of chat rooms and forums they visit.

Someone's digital footprint makes it possible to build up a picture of what kind of person they are. It shows things they are interested in, how many friends they have, the area where they live and how often they go on holiday, for example.

### THE KNOWLEDGE

Many websites use "**cookies**". A cookie is a simple file that a website transfers to your computer. Then, next time the computer visits the same site, the website remembers that you have visited it before. Examples of cookies in action could be websites knowing what kind of music you listened to, or what sort of video you watched, last time you visited them.

# CHAPTER 3: WHAT IS AN ONLINE IDENTITY?

▲Information like the kind of bands and music you like is part of your online identity.

A person's online identity is made up of all the information about them that other computer users can see. It isn't quite the same as a digital footprint: the whole of someone's digital footprint is only visible to computer experts using special tools.

## What is included in an online identity?

A digital identity can contain all kinds of information. Often it is based on popular **social networking** sites, which allow users to set up a **profile**. This could contain an **avatar**, information about where someone lives, their favourite websites, bands, books and lots more. Information on other sites, such as chat rooms or gaming sites, is also part of someone's online identity.

# THE KNOWLEDGE

Many countries have rules about the gathering of information about children. In the USA, for example, a law regulates the storage of information on under-13s. As a result, some websites do not allow children of 12 or younger to **register**. Rules such as this are there to protect young people. Pretending to be older than you are to get round the rules is a bad idea.

The information a person includes in their online identity is not necessarily true. Someone short could claim to be tall or say that they're a great dancer, when actually they are neither. A person could include a photograph of someone else and pretend it's them. They could lie about how old they are or almost anything else.

▲Any information a person shares online - that they love Britain's Royal Family, for example - becomes part of their online identity.

◀Whenever you set up any kind of internet account, or give out information, make sure an adult helps you decide what is safe to include.

## Public information

There are some kinds of information that most people don't mind other people knowing. For example, someone might not mind everyone knowing they are a Manchester United fan or that they love to watch old dance performances on the internet. It is usually fine to let this kind of information, which cannot be used to identify you, out on the internet.

## DO'S AND DON'TS

DO:      Think twice before releasing ANY information about yourself on the internet

DON'T:   Give out information that could be used to identify you or find out your location

# Private information

Information such as where someone lives, when they were born, or where they are going to be at a particular time should be kept private. NEVER make private information visible on the internet. (In fact, always check with a trusted adult whether it is alright to give any information to an internet site, even if it seems to be completely private.) Once information is released, you lose control of who knows it and who doesn't. You may think you've left your address where only people coming to your birthday party can see it, but it could still become public.

## Case study: tracking Dave Sandals

Here is a simple example of how someone's name and two facts can be used to track them down:

1. On a social networking site, someone called Dave Sandals says he lives in Brighton. One of his hobbies is surfing.

2. On another networking site, the tracker does a search for "Dave Sandals". Twenty-seven people with the same name pop up – but only one likes surfing! It is probably the same person. On this site, Dave has posted a message about how hard swimming training was on Tuesday evening.

The person investigating Dave now knows that he can probably be found at a Brighton swimming club on Tuesday evenings.

# Privacy settings

Most websites where people record information about themselves have privacy settings. These let the user control whether other people can see all of the information. A typical choice is:

• No one except you

• You and your friends

• You, your friends and their friends

• Everyone

The privacy settings are usually chosen when a person first **registers** with the website. They can still be changed later.

▲Would you want strangers to be able to see your private information? If not, do not share it!

## THE KNOWLEDGE

Before giving a website any information, it is a good idea to do some research into its privacy settings and how they work. Try this search term:

• [name of website] + privacy settings

Pages that are part of the website are not independent. Try to look at information on a page that is NOT part of the website you are researching.

# COMPUTER FUTURE

The development of wearable computers (see page 13) has made it possible for strangers walking along the street to get information about people they see. For example, a wearable with a camera uses face-recognition software to find out who someone is, then the computer searches for their online identity.

Just like in real life, it's best to share information only with people you know: your friends. It might be tempting to include their friends too – but you don't actually know them, so how can you be sure you want them to know all about you?

Privacy settings are a useful tool – but it is important to remember that once something is posted on a website and anyone else has access to it, it could quickly spread around the internet. All someone has to do is copy and paste it

## Choose your privacy settings

|  | Everyone | Friends of friends | Friends only |
|---|---|---|---|
| Profile |  |  | ✔ |
| Birthday |  |  | ✔ |
| Family |  |  | ✔ |
| Relationships |  |  | ✔ |
| Phone number and address |  |  | ✔ |
| Photos |  |  | ✔ |

▲Letting everyone see your status or information is a very bad idea.

▲Lots of people use their pet's name as a password. While this is easy to remember, it is also easily guessed!

## Passwords

The most important way of keeping information safe is by using a password. To access their information, computer users have to **log in** – usually by giving their email address and password.

If someone else guesses or finds your password, they can pretend to be you. This is called **identity theft**. Never share a password with anyone. The only other person who should know it is your parent or guardian, who will have helped set it up.

### THE KNOWLEDGE

Many websites have a tickbox labelled "Remember me" or "Stay signed in". Ticking this means that next time the computer visits that site, the site will assume the same person has come back. Un-ticking the box makes sure someone else cannot come along later and use the computer pretending to be you.

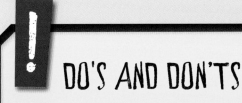

## DO'S AND DON'TS

DO: Make a password a hard-to-guess nonsense word

DON'T: Write passwords down

# WORST PASSWORDS

| Rank | Password |
| --- | --- |
| #1 | password |
| #2 | 123456 |
| #3 | 12345678 |
| #4 | abc123 |
| #5 | qwerty |
| #6 | monkey |
| #7 | letmein |
| #8 | dragon |
| #9 | 111111 |
| #10 | baseball |

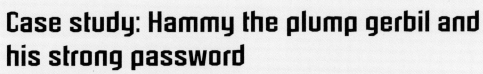

## Case study: Hammy the plump gerbil and his strong password

1. A password is "strong" if it is difficult to guess. The best password is a nonsense word that will still be easy to remember. For example, you might have a slightly overweight pet gerbil with brown ears, called Hammy.

2. Make a sentence of this: "Hammy is round and has brown ears."

3. Take the first letter of each word: HIRAHBE.

4. Change two of the letters for numbers: I could become 1, and A could become a 4.

5. This produces the password H1R4HBE. Hammy's owner can remember it easily, but no one else will be able to guess it.

6. The basic password can be adapted to any website. Just add the first letter of the website's name to the start of the password, and the last letter to the end. So for Yoursphere, the password would become yH1R4HBEe.

# Cyber strangers

People you do not know, who try to introduce themselves on the internet, are called cyber strangers. Just like IRL, contact with a stranger can lead to danger. The same rules apply in the digital world: be wary of contact from strangers, and tell an adult about the contact straight away.

On a computer, it is harder to tell if someone is a dangerous stranger. They might have hidden behind a **false identity**. For example, someone who says they are a 10-year-old girl from Los Angeles could *actually* be a 53-year-old man from London. Some strangers even pretend to be someone you know. They appear on the screen under the same name, or a very similar one, but are actually somebody else.

▲One advantage of computer wearables (see page 13) might be that you'll be able to tell if people have described themselves honestly!

## THE KNOWLEDGE

1. Cyber danger-strangers will ask for personal details such as your name, age or whether you are a boy or girl.
2. They agree with you about everything: this is a way of getting you to trust them.
3. They want to meet up in person.
4. They are weirdly nice, for example always saying how brilliant or funny your replies are.

## Case study: Brooke and the stranger Chantelle

Brooke and Chantelle are friends. They sometimes chat on an internet forum. One night, Brooke gets a message from Chantele:

Chantele: Hey, Brooke, what's up?

Brooke: Homework!

Chantele: Drag! Where are you up to?

Brooke: Last question... hard one!

Chantele: Me too. Want to meet at Katz's later?

Brooke then rings Chantelle, and finds out the messages aren't from her at all. A stranger has been trying to arrange to meet Brooke by pretending to be Chantelle. Brooke goes to tell her mum.

From the beginning, there was a clue that it was a stranger. What was it?

Answer: Look at how the stranger appears onscreen. Chantelle's name has a letter missing.

▶ On the internet, people are not always exactly what they say they are.

## DO'S AND DON'TS

DO: tell an adult about messages from people you don't know

DON'T: arrange meetings on the internet: unwelcome people could see the details and turn up at the meeting

# CHAPTER 4: CAN YOU TELL IF A WEB PAGE IS SAFE TO VISIT?

◀A trusted adult - a relative or a teacher, for example - will be able to tell you if a new website is safe to use.

Some web pages look normal but are really a cover for something else. They might be trying to persuade people to give up their personal information, or the website could be trying to download **malware** that will damage your computer.

## Doing research

Before giving a web page any information, it is best to do some research on whether other people have had problems with it. An internet search using the terms "[site name]" + "reviews" should reveal what other people think of it, and whether they have had any problems.

## THE KNOWLEDGE

Usernames are the names people give themselves on websites. The best usernames do not contain personal information. Someone's real name (e.g. 'jademciver') or an activity they like ('gymnasticsgirl') makes a bad username.

# Asking why information is needed

If a website asks for information, you should question why they need it. For example, to join a chat room users normally have to give a **username**, an email address, and a password. This is reasonable: users need a username, plus a password for protection (see page 22). The people who run the site need an email address for the user.

A chat room does *not* need to know someone's full name and address, or their passwords for other sites (for example). If it asks for these, it is best to leave the site immediately.

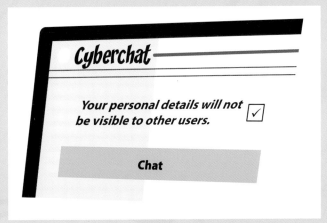

**Cyberchat**

*Your personal details will not be visible to other users.* ☑

**Chat**

▲Any personal details you give when registering with websites such as chat rooms will not be seen by other users.

## DO'S AND DON'TS

DO:    Ask an adult to help you whenever you are asked to put *any* personal information into a computer

DON'T:  Assume that because a website looks professional, it must be safe. This isn't always the case

# ✓ 24-7Anti-virus

## ⊖ !WARNING!

## Malware detected

◄Computers have some defences against malware.

## Malware

Malware is short for **MALicious** softWARE. Malware can be harmful in several ways. It can gather information secretly, cause the computer to stop working, or be used to spy on the computer's user. Malware is sometimes downloaded secretly from web pages, or after a computer's user clicks a **link** in an email.

## DO'S AND DON'TS

DO: Check whether a computer's malware protection is up to date (ask an adult to help)

DON'T: Click on links in emails unless you are sure they are not malware. Hover your cursor over the link, without clicking on it: a web address should appear. Is it different from what you expect? For example, an email from Apple should link to a simple apple.com web address. If the address that actually appears is "jaycophish9119.co.au", it's not a real Apple email.

## THE KNOWLEDGE

Some of the key types of malware are:

- Keyloggers: hidden programmes that record everything that is typed using a computer keyboard.
- Spyware: malware that secretly gathers information about a computer's user.
- Trojan horses: programmes that allow someone secret access to a computer, often causing information to be wiped out.
- Viruses: malware that, once it has entered a computer, becomes part of the programmes that are already installed. The virus then tries to spread to other computers in the same network.
- Worms: malware that spreads itself between computers, but without becoming part of programmes that are already installed.

## Protection from malware

Computers can be protected from malware in several ways. The simplest is never to connect the computer to the internet, which is where almost all malware comes from. For computers that are connected to the internet, the diagram below shows how most malware is defeated before it even reaches a computer. The final line of defence is the malware-protection software most computers are fitted with. This flashes up a warning if it notices suspicious activity.

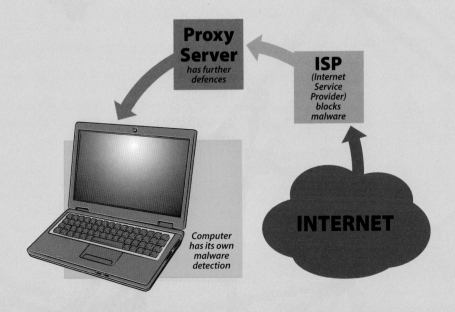

**Proxy Server** *has further defences*

**ISP** *(Internet Service Provider) blocks malware*

*Computer has its own malware detection*

**INTERNET**

# CHAPTER 5: WHAT IS COMPUTER ETIQUETTE?

◀Being unkind or rude using a computer is just as upsetting for the victim - and just as wrong - as it would be in real life.

Etiquette is a word that describes the rules for behaving correctly and treating other people well. Computer etiquette means behaving correctly when using a computer. It especially applies to the internet, or net – so some people call it *netiquette*.

## THE KNOWLEDGE

Every computer has an IP address, which is like a digital fingerprint (see page 14). Just like real fingerprints, these can be used to track down wrongdoers – even people hiding behind a false identity.

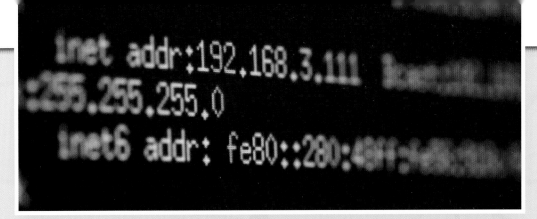

▲This image shows part of a computer's IP address. It can be used to track what the computer has been used for.

# Bad behaviour

Some computer users forget that there are real people, whose feelings can be hurt, behind the names that appear on a chat room or forum. They think it is OK to be rude or unkind. This is wrong. Firstly, it is never acceptable to be rude or inconsiderate to someone else. Secondly, although people might think that others don't know who they are and they can get away with it, it is actually quite simple to identify someone. It can be done through the details they supplied when they joined the chat room, or in other, more technical ways. (See The Knowledge panel on page 30 for one of these.)

## THE KNOWLEDGE

On a computer message, the person receiving the message cannot hear the voice or see the facial expressions of the person sending it. This can lead to misunderstanding and upset.

Adding an emoticon is a fast way to make the meaning of a message clearer. Here are some common ones:

| | | | |
|---|---|---|---|
| :) | happy | :(( | really unhappy |
| :D | smiling | :'( | shedding a tear |
| :P | joking or disgusted | :O | surprised |
| :( | unhappy | | |

Most computers come supplied with emoticons that can be added to messages, but if not, the keyboard versions shown above can be used.

## THE KNOWLEDGE

This is a three-step guide to dealing with internet trolls:

1. Ignore the troll. They love attention, and if they do not get it, they often go away.
2. Report the troll to the web page's **moderators**, so that they can watch his or her behaviour.
3. Ask the moderator to block the troll, so that he or she can't post any more comments.

# Beware of the trolls!

On the internet, a troll is someone who is rude, objectionable, and unkind to other internet users. Everyone who uses the internet, especially forums or chat rooms, eventually comes across a troll. Trolls get their name because they like to lie in wait (like a fairytale troll hiding under a bridge), before launching a sudden, unexpected attack.

# Signs you have met a troll

1. Trolls like to claim that what they think is fact – even though it is really just the troll's opinion.

2. Trolls never admit they are wrong, or that anyone else has a right to a different opinion.

3. Trolls don't care about hurting other people's feelings. If someone else gets angry or upset, the troll gets extra satisfaction.

4. Trolls carry on arguing even when it is obvious they are wrong and no one agrees with them.

Fortunately, trolls are attention seekers. If ignored, they usually go away.

**Real life:**

**Internet:**

# Fighting bad computer etiquette

It would be great if everyone on the internet always showed kindness and respect towards other people. Unfortunately, though, this is not the case. When people do behave badly, it is usually possible to stop them.

## On a forum

If people can post comments, the forum will have a moderator. If enough people complain to the moderator, he or she can:

• delete offensive comments

• contact the offender asking them to change their behaviour

• block the user from posting comments at all.

## DO'S AND DON'TS

DO: Always be polite and kind

DON'T: Say anything you would not say in the middle of a crowded shopping mall, where everyone can hear

DO: Remember that anything you write *could* be spread around. Imagine a parent or teacher reading your words – would they approve?

DON'T: Forget that once something is on the internet, it could still be visible years later

DO: Respect other people's opinions

DON'T: Use capital letters the whole time – it is like shouting at someone. I SAID DON'T USE CAPITALS!

## instantMessage

*This comment has been deleted because it fails to comply with community standards.*

### By mobile phone or instant messaging

Most smartphones let users block unwelcome messages and calls, just by tapping "Block" on the menu. If it is not clear how to do this, the phone company will be able to help.

For instant messaging, users can set things up so that only people on their contacts list can get in touch. Ask an adult to help you with setting up these systems.

### On a website

If something on a website is offensive, either the **host administrator** or the **ISP** can be contacted. They can then remove the website. If something on a website is illegal, it may be best to contact the police.

### THE KNOWLEDGE

A web page's "host" is where it lives on the Internet. Hosts are like office buildings: they provide the web page with space to put information. Normally the host does not look at what the information is. If someone complains, though, the host can tell the web page to go away.

# Protecting other people

Computer etiquette is about how computer users behave themselves, and also how they treat other people. An important part of this is being careful with other people's information, particularly their contact details. Releasing someone's address, phone number or email, for example, could put them in danger.

## Case study: Tina and Louise

Tina met a boy at a gymnastics competition. He asked for her email, to send her a link to a video of a fantastic routine. Tina knew she shouldn't give out her private details – so she gave the boy her friend Louise's email instead. Louise ended up getting lots of unwelcome messages from the boy and was really upset. In the end, she had to change her email address.

# Online money

It is possible to buy and sell almost everything on the internet – from groceries to music to **apps**. People can record their payment details, to make paying faster next time. This can lead to problems when more than one person uses the same computer.

For example, some games offer players the chance to make **in-app** purchases that will make the game more fun. If a new player starts the game, he or she must be careful not to agree to improvements that the computer's owner will have to pay for.

## DO'S AND DON'TS

DO:     Always check with a computer's owner before agreeing to any updates

DON'T: Ever agree to any downloads that the computer's owner might have to pay for

# CHAPTER 6: CYBER BULLYING

"Cyber" means to do with computers. Cyber bullies use a computer to pick on someone and make them feel scared or unhappy. The computer could be a desktop, a mobile phone, or any of the other devices listed on page 7.

◄ Cyber bullying has driven some people to despair. It is just as bad as bullying in the non-computer world.

## Examples of cyber bullying

- Sending nasty or threatening messages, or making aggressive comments.

- Posting embarrassing photos or videos of someone where everyone can see them.

- Making someone feel they are being hunted by constantly sending them messages.

- Setting up fake profiles that make fun of someone and are unkind about them.

- Sharing or forwarding someone's messages, personal information or photos without their permission.

Cyber bullies sometimes prefer to act anonymously. Not knowing who their tormentor is makes the victim feel even worse.

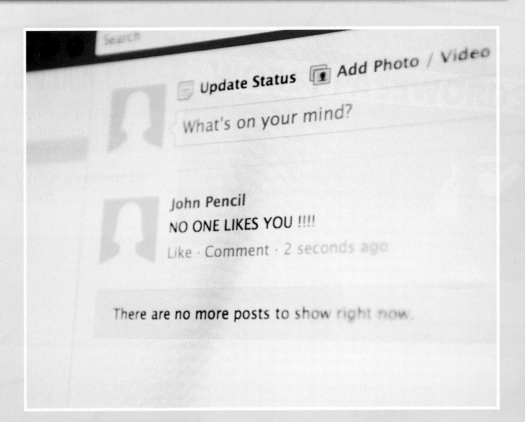

Search

Update Status    Add Photo / Video

What's on your mind?

**John Pencil**
NO ONE LIKES YOU !!!!
Like · Comment · 2 seconds ago

There are no more posts to show right now.

## THE KNOWLEDGE

Bullying of any kind, whether it is done using computers or not, is a shameful way to behave. It could also be illegal:

1. Most countries have laws against harassment (threatening or tormenting someone).

2. It may also be illegal to use the telephone system (which is what the internet uses to communicate) for improper actions.

## DO'S AND DON'TS

DO:    Think about whether what you say in messages or posts could hurt someone's feelings

DON'T: Join in when you see someone else being bullied

▲ Just like bullying IRL, cyber bullying should always be reported to a trusted adult.

## Avoiding cyber bullies

How can people stop cyber bullies in their tracks? The best way is to make it impossible for a bully to get hold of you in the first place. No one can send unpleasant phone messages or emails if they do not know the number or email to use. Family and close friends are the only people who need this information.

Cyber bullies find it harder to pick on someone who keeps their information private. For example, people who send out lots of photos of themselves messing about are an easy target. All the bully has to do is add a nasty description or some artwork, and the person in the picture is humiliated.

## THE KNOWLEDGE

There are websites that you can visit for more information and advice on cyber bullying.

**www.beatbullying.org**
Young people who've experienced bullying can help each other or talk to an online **mentor**.

**www.chatdanger.com**
chatdanger gives information and advice about cyber bullying and other computer-safety issues.

**www.digizen.org/kids**
Click through to "let's fight it together", an award-winning film about cyber bullying.

## DO'S AND DON'TS

DO:    Keep any bullying messages, plus **screen grabs** of bullying posts. It is tempting to delete hurtful messages, but they are evidence

DON'T: Reply to cyber bullying

DO:    Ask an adult to help you block messages and emails from the bully

DON'T: Suffer in silence. Always tell an adult about bullying: parents and teachers, for example, will be able to help

DO:    Get an adult to report bullying to the forum moderator and/or mobile-phone company

# CONCLUSION: TIPS FOR ONLINE SAFETY

Using a computer safely is relatively easy for anyone who follows a few simple, general rules. Computer users shouldn't do anything in the digital world that they wouldn't do IRL. They should not write anything that they would not like to see pinned to a public noticeboard. They should always treat other people as they would want to be treated themselves.

## Computer Use Agreement

1. Together, my parents and I will agree the rules for when and how I can use the internet. I will stick to these rules!

2. I will not give out addresses, real names, or contact details of any kind unless a parent says it is OK.

3. I will not post photos of myself or other people without a parent's approval.

4. I will tell a trusted adult straight away if anything on a computer makes me feel uncomfortable or unhappy.

5. I will treat other people on the internet as I would treat them IRL.

6. I will never arrange a meeting using the computer or meet up with someone I don't already know IRL.

7. The only people who will ever know my passwords are my parents and me.

8. I will not download anything to the computer without permission.

9. I will not reply to messages that are unkind or rude – but I will tell a trusted adult about them.

10. I will try to educate my parents about the internet, computers and technology.

# GLOSSARY

**apps** short for "applications", computer programmes that perform specific jobs (such as telling you the weather, or gathering together the news)

**avatar** image used to represent someone in the computer world. A person's avatar could be based on their real appearance, or it could look completely different.

**chat room** internet page where people "talk" to each other by typing messages

**cloud storage** storage of information that is not on a computer's own hard drive. Instead, the computer sends the information to another hard drive. It is a bit like putting boxes of papers in a garage, instead of keeping them in your bedroom.

**cookie** simple file transferred from a website to a computer. The cookie allows the website to recognise the computer the next time the two are connected.

**digital** involving computers

**download** process of transferring something from the internet on to your personal computer or smartphone

**false identity** pretending to be someone you are not, usually a completely made-up person

**futurist** person who tries to work out what the future is going to be like

**host administrator** person who looks after the computer (server) where a website is stored

**identity theft** pretending to be someone else, usually in order to steal their information or money

**illegal** not allowed and punishable by the police

**in-app** part of an app (application). For example, buying a new pair of sneakers for your character in a game would be an in-app purchase.

**inappropriate** not suitable, likely to hurt or offend someone

**IRL** short for In Real Life

**ISP** short for Internet Service Provider, the company that provides internet access. ISPs are often phone companies.

**link** short for "hyperlink", a word or image that, when clicked on, will take you to an internet page

**log in** give a password and other details to an internet page so that it recognises your computer

**malicious** nasty and dangerous

**malware** computer programmes designed to harm other people's computers or their users in some way

**mentor** guide or counsellor; someone who listens and, if asked, gives advice

**modem** device that allows a computer to be connected to the internet

**moderator** person on an internet site who decides whether people's comments and behaviour are unacceptable

**offline** not connected to the internet

**online** connected to the internet

**profile** information about a computer user that is stored on an internet site

**proxy server** computer that makes it easier for two other computers to speak to each other

**register** join, by providing details about yourself

**router** device that allows more than one computer to use a single internet connection

**screen grab** stored image of what is on a computer screen at a particular moment. Even if the screen later changes, what it used to say is visible in the screen grab.

**settings** controls for how a computer works and which information its user wants to share with other people

**social networking** using a computer to link with other people

**software** computer application or program designed to do a specific task, for example send email (Outlook), edit photos (Photoshop) or record music (GarageBand)

**upload** process of transferring something from your computer to a website or file server

**username** name someone uses on the internet. Some people have different names on different internet pages.

**website** collection of writing, pictures, music and sound that is stored on a computer and made available to everyone on the internet

**wireless** technology that allows the exchange of information, but does not require traditional cables or wires

# FIND OUT MORE

## Books

*Cyber Bullying* Nick Hunter (Raintree, 2011)

*Cyber Bullying* Heather E Schwartz (Capstone Press, 2014)

*Internet Safety* Nick Hunter (Raintree, 2011)

*Safe Social Networking* Heather E Schwartz (Capstone Press, 2014)

*A Smart Girl's Guide to the Internet* Sharon Miller Cindrich (American Girl Publishing, 2009)

*A Smart Kid's Guide to Internet Privacy* David J Jakubiak (PowerKids Press, 2009)

## Websites

### Bullying

There are three excellent internet resources where you can find information and advice about bullying listed on page 41 (beatbullying.org, chatdanger.net and digizen.org/kids).

### Internet safety

www.childnet.com/young-people

This section of the childnet site is aimed specifically at young people. There is advice on protecting your online reputation, safe social networking, apps, downloads, and lots more.

www.kidsmart.org.uk

The kidsmart site has information for kids, parents and teachers on internet safety. The kids' bit has sections on digital footprints, smartphones, chat, photos, social networking, music and more.

http://www.nsteens.org/

Comics, games, videos and more: it hardly seems like learning about internet safety at all, but this is an excellent site. It's really aimed at teenagers, but could be used by younger children too.

## Places to visit

*The National Museum of Computing, Milton Keynes, UK*

This museum is at Bletchley Park, where during the Second World War British and the US began to develop the first computers. There are displays and information about these early efforts, as well as later developments in computing.

# INDEX